THE For-Profit Grant Writing Guide

THE STORY OF ONE COMPANY'S

TRANSFORMATION BY USING THE

FUNDING EQUATION

Micki Vandeloo, GPC

ISBN: 150035032X
ISBN 13: 9781500350321
Library of Congress Control Number: 2014911868
CreateSpace Independent Publishing Platform
North Charleston, South Carolina

TABLE OF CONTENTS

INTRODUCTION

"I can't justify this investment. The return on investment (ROI) just isn't there."

"I would love to have that piece of equipment, but I really can't afford it."

"Yes, recycling is good for the environment. We would love to recycle our used plastic. But recycling is also expensive, and we don't have that money lying around."

In over twenty years of working in and around for-profit companies in a variety of consulting, grant writing, sales, and leadership capacities, I have heard all of the above statements and more.

It is a constant conundrum for for-profit organizations. The leaders and C-level managers want to invest in employees and equipment. They want to train employees. They want to do what is right for the environment. But when pencil meets paper, the numbers just don't add up.

Let's play a game of "what if."

What if there were a way to reduce the investment in equipment and training? Wouldn't that increase ROI? *What if* the new ROI made the investment more palatable for a company?

What if that company were able to justify the purchase of said equipment and made this investment? *What if* productivity increased as a result of the new equipment? *What if* there were increases in both the amount of product shipped and the product's sales numbers?

What if ten new employees were hired to meet the demand for the product produced on the new machinery? Wouldn't the local economy gain from the increased employment?

What if this same scenario played out at a thousand companies? Imagine the economic impact that would result!

What if I told you that grant funding is the key to the initial cost reduction that led to the justification of the equipment purchase and the resulting huge economic impact?

Would you say, "Well, that's all well and good, but I wouldn't know where to start looking for grant funding. And even if I knew where to look, I wouldn't be able to do the work to access it"?

If so, this book is for you!

I will start in Chapter 1 by dispelling some of the myths associated with grants and grant writing. The next chapter, "Conducting Effective Grant Research," will explain the funding equation and one particularly important component of it. Chapter 3 will discuss the basic elements of a grant application. The final chapter will provide some tips for improving the probability of a successful grant application and reporting process.

This book uses some manufacturing terms and analogies, as that is where much of my experience with for-profit grant funding lies. However, the tools, techniques and tips discussed in this book apply to any for-profit grant research and application process.

To help those not in manufacturing understand the whole book's context, allow me to define the terms specific to that sector below:

- Equipment – This is defined in the world of grants as a depreciable item or something with a value over $5,000. This could be a new machine, or office equipment if you are a start up company applying for a grant. For the purposes of this book and the case study, the word equipment refers to manufacturing equipment.
- Lean Manufacturing – A set of tools that can be used by companies in any industry sector to eliminate non-value added or wasteful activities.
- TS16949 – A quality standard used by the automotive industry that outlines requirements for quality systems and procedures to ensure a robust management and quality structure for companies in the automotive supply base.

My goal in writing this book isn't to make you an expert grant researcher and writer. My goal is to help you understand the process, know when and where to keep your eyes and ears open for funding opportunities, and comprehend the role you and your team can play to make your next grant application a successful one. I hope that you will keep this on your bookshelf as a reference if you have any questions about funding a potential project.

To illustrate the concepts, I have included a case study from a fictional manufacturing company. You may find that your company is in the same or a similar situation.

Also, I included a page for you to take notes after each chapter. I hope that the content generates some great project ideas or thoughts. I want you to be able to capture your innovation and creativity right in this book for future reference.

Common Grant Writing Definitions

Before we delve into the big world of grant funding, it is necessary to understand a couple of common grant writing industry terms: *funder* and *grant*.

A **funder** (or **funding source** or **funding agency**) is an organization that distributes grant money. Funders can be foundations; federal, state, or local government departments (such as a department of economic development); or colleges.

A **grant** (or **funding**) is a sum of money provided for a specific purpose. A company or organization submits a request for grant money, typically via an application. The funder then reviews the application and either approves or denies the request. If the funder approves the request, the funder then distributes money to the applicant via a single check or series of checks.

DRI Case Study

To illustrate the concepts in this book, I will use the case of an imaginary company called Do Right Inc. (DRI for short).

> DRI (Do Right Inc.) is owned by a woman named Sue and employs twenty-five associates in a rural area. DRI currently runs one shift of production, but Sue is interested in growing the business to be able to hire more people from the community.
>
> DRI manufactures plastic parts for the automotive industry using an injection molding process. They operate three presses and a paint line, as well as ancillary assembly and trimming operations. The rejected parts are sent to a grinder, and some of the reground plastic is reused for production of additional parts. However, due to customer restrictions on the amount of reground plastic used in the products, they have excess reground plastic that cannot be reused and currently send to a landfill for disposal.
>
> During the most recent strategic planning process, Sue and her management team brainstormed ways to grow the business and use the excess plastic to avoid costly disposal fees. The sales team continues to pursue some exciting options with both current and new customers to get more of the current product line into the automotive markets. However, the sales manager has been doing some research and has discovered an opportunity to grow their business by offering components for the renewable energy industry. Using the current molding machines and the balance of the reground plastic inventory, the company can mold parts for solar panel production. A new mold and packaging line would be required to start production. The antiquated, inefficient grinder also needs to be replaced, as

the maintenance costs are starting to outweigh the cost of a new grinder. New grinders are also more energy efficient.

According to the sales manager, there are already three new customers ready to buy the components, so this is a great opportunity to better utilize the equipment. If the projected sales come to fruition, entry into the solar market is projected to increase sales by 30 percent (after recouping the initial equipment investment) and eventually result in three new packing jobs, two more office positions, and a seven-person crew to run the presses for an additional shift. The new employees and some current employees will have to be trained to operate the press and to run the new packaging line.

To improve throughput and productivity as the operation grows, the company has decided to implement a structured continuous improvement program. Sue intends to have all of her employees trained on the basics of Lean Manufacturing. She is going to work with a local consulting organization to teach employees about these tools and techniques to streamline operations and reduce waste.

Sue also plans to pursue TS16949 quality certification to satisfy her automotive customers' requirements. Internal auditors will need to be trained, and the system will be developed using a provider from a local community college and a team of her employees. This training is considered essential for expanding their penetration in the automotive market.

However, when the Engineering Manager gives Sue the equipment investment estimate, she goes into sticker shock.

New plastic grinding machine	$400,000
New molds for parts for the solar industry	$300,000
New packaging line for solar industry parts	$225,000
Total equipment investment	**$925,000**

When she reviews the quotes for the Lean Manufacturing and quality system training, her stomach turns. The total training cost is expected to amount to seventy-five thousand dollars.

A total investment of one million dollars? Sue puts her head in her hands. She really wants to move forward with these projects based on their potential, but based on discussions with her financial advisor and her salesperson, the payback on the investment is over three years. She just can't justify the expenditure based on this ROI. When Sue started the company, she vowed never to make an investment unless the payback period was two years or less. She intends to keep that promise to herself.

Sue is proud of the way her company has supported the rural community by employing its residents. She values her employees and the strong work ethic they show. She knows that by expanding the company's capabilities and improving her employees' skill levels, she will be able to take her organization to another level of sales and customer service. She is also concerned about the environment, and the ability to reuse the excess reground plastic and grow her business at the same time really excites her.

What to do?

Sue remembers hearing about a grant writer who specializes in helping for-profit companies obtain funding for their projects.

She rifles through her desk drawer and finds the consultant's business card, which a fellow business owner had given her at a recent Rotary Club meeting. Sue picks up the phone and dials the writer's number. Maybe this is the answer she's looking for!

Chapter 1

GRANT WRITING MYTHS AND
MISCONCEPTIONS

In my years of grant writing and consulting, I have repeatedly seen the shocked looks on clients' faces when I tell them that they may be able to access grant funding for an upcoming equipment or training investment. In the conversations that follow, however, many grant myths and misconceptions come to light. These mistruths often keep company leaders from pursuing grant funding. Before we can address the grant research and writing process, I must dispel these myths.

———

Myth 1: Grant funding is "free money."

When I mention grant funding to most company leaders, their first reaction is, "I want some of that free money!" I have to say, my skin crawls at the mention of the term "free money."

I know where this misconception originates. Because grant funding is not a loan, there are no interest charges or required payback schedules for a grant. Therefore, the money is, in a sense, free. There are, however, costs associated with the grant writing process.

These sometimes well-hidden expenses include time and exposure.

Time

Properly researching, writing, and administering a grant takes time. There are costs associated with that time.

In the case of companies who use internal resources to conduct these activities, there is an employee's salary and benefits for the time he or she spends on grant writing activities. If the employee doesn't know anything about grant writing, there will be additional time spent training that employee to get up to speed on the grant writing process. Many companies also don't consider the opportunity cost of shifting employees away from the jobs that they have been trained to do in order to research, write grants, and perform the post-award administrative tasks.

Organizations can avoid many of the above costs by hiring a freelance grant professional. A good grant professional will be able to efficiently and quickly identify sources of grant funding (if they exist), compile an application, and assist with grant reporting and evaluation activities. While it does cost money to hire an outside resource, many companies find that it is ultimately much cheaper and less time-consuming to do so than to use internal resources.

Exposure

In order to obtain grant funding, companies will often have to open their books and, in some cases, their doors, to funders.

Documents commonly requested by funders during the grant application process include:

- financial statements (current and two to three years in the past);
- employee wages, including those of top management;
- an organizational chart or other information on the board of directors and company management structure; and
- key employees' résumés.

Privately held companies may have have reservations about supplying these documents, particularly to government funding organizations. It has been my experience that funders are inflexible on these requirements. They need to know that the company is stable and well-run and that it doesn't have millions of dollars lying around to pay for the project. Just as your bank requires information to issue a loan, if a funder is going to give you hundreds of thousands, even millions, of dollars to help pay for equipment or training, you must provide full disclosure.

In addition, if you receive a grant, particularly one associated with a government entity, you may be asked (possibly more than once during the grant term) to host a tour or press conference for politicians. While most companies don't particularly enjoy this type of activity, political officials love to appear to be "in the trenches." The larger the grant, the more likely these visits are to take place.

Finally, most grant programs require an audit during or after the grant project. You must be prepared to show documentation of expenditures and make all project information available to the auditors.

———

Myth 2: Writing a grant is no harder than writing a letter.

When company leaders find out about grant funding opportunities, many times their first inclination is to assign the grant writing duties to an administrative assistant or a human resources (HR) manager or staff member, thinking that writing a grant is no harder than compiling a report or a letter. On the contrary, unless these employees have experience writing grants, they will have an uphill battle to fight.

Grant funding applications have very specific requirements, which we will discuss in more detail in chapter 4. One of the most complicated portions of a grant application is the narrative. In this section of the grant application, you will:

- introduce your company;
- state the need that is being met by the project for which you are seeking funding;
- explain how the project meets that need;
- identify the resources you will dedicate to the project;
- document your project plan, including the method you will use to evaluate its effectiveness and the project schedule; and
- outline the budget for the project.

To complicate matters, the narrative has page and format limitations. Not adhering to the content and formatting requirements will get an otherwise well-written grant application thrown out by the funder in a heartbeat.

Acquiring the information for the narrative requires coordination and project management skills. The HR department commonly has to supply wage information and hiring plans. The engineering department may have input for the project plan and the budget. The production floor must provide input on timing to install equipment or conduct training, as these tasks affect production schedules. The finance department clearly plays a role in developing the budget. The coordination required to put together an effective grant application can require more skills and time than a staff member is willing or able to commit.

In addition, the narrative must flow and clearly tie the stated need to the solution that the project proposes. Business and technical writing skills are often necessary to concisely and accurately complete the narrative, particularly for capital equipment projects.

Underestimating the skills required to write a successful grant application is common. However, doing so can result in added stress for your staff. It may also lead to rejection of your application, sometimes for something as seemingly meaningless as using the wrong font. Then all that time, effort, and money are wasted.

———

Myth 3: Getting a grant solves all your problems.

One of my saddest experiences as a grant writer is helping a company obtain funding and then watching the project fail. When you submit a grant application, there is a defined project for which the funding will be used. If your company gets funding, you will sign an agreement stating that you will complete the project. If you don't do so according to plan, the funding agency can refuse to pay you part or all of the grant money or even force you to refund money you have received.

When this happens, management often questions the value of the grant and maybe even the grant writer. In my experience, any of the following situations can result in project failure:

- poor project planning
- poor project management
- lack of project support from C-level managers
- faulty or nonexistent company communications about the project's status or goals
- lack of financial systems to appropriately track expenditures
- lack of a strategic plan to align the project with the organization's mission

As you can see, none of the above reasons are associated with the actual grant writing process or the person writing the application.

————

What if Sue from our case study company, DRI, had bought into any or all of the myths above?

- She may have greatly underestimated the cost of a strong grant writing effort and used internal staff to research and write the grants. Her staff would have been stressed by the amount of effort they were being asked to put forth to accommodate funder questions, visits and tours. Productivity would have declined, and morale would have suffered.
- She may have assigned the grant writing and research tasks to her administrative assistant, Jane, who had no experience in grant writing. Jane would have spent hours looking for grant funding, and Sue's administrative tasks would have been left undone. Jane would also have spent days writing and rewriting a grant application. The application would have been less likely to be approved due to Jane's lack of grant writing expertise. In the end, both

Sue and Jane's productivity would have suffered, and they may have had nothing to show for the effort.

- Sue's projects were definitely aligned with her strategic plan. However, her new engineering manager (who replaced a recently retired company veteran) may have inaccurately specified the equipment and greatly underestimated the timing. Due to poor project planning, the grant may have been rescinded due to lack of performance to the application's stated project plan. No funding and useless equipment: not a great end to the story.

Fortunately, Sue's grant writer addressed all of these potential pitfalls and managed a solid effort (to be discussed in further detail in the next section) at planning the project and researching and writing the grant, so that none of these issues actually occurred.

Unfortunately, I have seen and read about situations like the ones just described. When company leaders believe the grant myths and misconceptions, the results can be devastating for the company and its employees.

NOTES

Chapter 2

CONDUCTING EFFECTIVE

GRANT RESEARCH

I believe in simplification. To that end, I have developed an equation to help you remember the three key activities for accessing grant funding:

$$P + R + A = \$$$

P refers to a well-defined **project**.

R refers to grant **research**, and more specifically, *effective* grant research.

A refers to a well-written grant **application**.

And, of course, **$** is money for your next project!

This chapter will address P and R equation elements. Chapter 3, Elements of a Typical Grant Application, will help explain grant applications and provide some techniques for writing a grant application that results in funding.

The Most Important Part of the Funding Equation

Now that we have cleared up the myths and misconceptions associated with grant funding, you are ready to embark on the grant research and writing process with your eyes wide open. The next two chapters will help you understand the project planning, grant research, and grant writing processes.

While the elements of the funding equation are important, the order of these events is also significant. You *must* have a well-defined project before you even begin the funding search. Good planning will save you immense amounts of time researching and applying for funding that isn't really a good fit for your project.

What, you may ask, is a well-defined project? It starts with a good project planning team. This group should consist of representatives from each department affected by the initiative.

The following departments should be represented on the typical for-profit planning team on an as-required basis:

- finance
- operations
- grant writing
- sales
- executive management
- engineering
- collaborating organizations

To be most effective, the project group should not consist of more than ten associates.

The first order of business is to identify the project leader. This person will conduct the following activities during project planning, grant research, grant application, and project execution:

- schedule and lead project planning team meetings
- ensure that the team's questions are addressed
- ensure that the funder's questions are addressed in a timely manner
- review the grant research results with the team
- ensure that funding requirements are clearly outlined for the group
- lead the evaluation of the potential funding programs, based on the research
- manage the grant writing efforts during the application process
- ensure that the project outcomes are met or exceeded

The project leader *must* answer funders' or potential funders' questions in a timely and accurate fashion. The project leader must be accessible and knowledgeable about the project. If funders don't get timely and knowledgable answers to their questions during the application process, the applicant will be in jeopardy of losing the grant money.

Once the team is formed, the project leader must call a project planning meeting (or series of meetings) to properly define the effort. Planning the project as a group ensures buy-in from all stakeholders for the initiative.

To help you conduct the most effective project definition meeting, I have created a list of elements required for a well-defined project. I recommend that you create a template incorporating the items below for your future planning efforts.

- **Project leader.** You will put the name of the person whom you identified as the project leader as the first order of business. DRI's project leader could be Sue, the company owner. However, if Sue travels frequently or isn't diligent about returning phone calls or e-mails, the engineering manager, HR manager, or grant writer may be better suited for this role. In this case, the grant writer was chosen as the project leader to allow Sue to continue to address the day-to-day needs of her business during the grant research and writing process.
- **Project name.** This should be a short title that effectively describes the project. This is not only a reference to the project for internal staff; it may also be the project name that you will use on grant applications. For the DRI case study, the project name might be "Equipment Purchase and Employee Training to Support Market Expansion."
- **Project description.** This is a short description of the project activities. A sample project description for the DRI case study might read:

  > Do Right Inc. (DRI) plans to purchase equipment and tooling to support market expansion into renewable energy and additional automotive markets. Employee training in continuous improvement methods and equipment operation will ensure that DRI's employees are prepared to respond to both current and new customer requirements in a timely and efficient manner. DRI also plans to implement a TS16949 quality system to address the needs of its current automotive customer base and to gain additional automotive market share.

- **Need addressed.** This is typically much more difficult for for-profit companies to define than for nonprofits. However, every project in either business segment has to address a company or regional need. For example, DRI's project addresses the company's need to expand its markets and increase the diversity of its customer base, the region's need for job growth, and its customers' needs for a quality program that meets a recognized industry standard. If your organization has a strategic plan, the project should meet at least some of the threats and weaknesses identified in the plan's SWOT (strengths, weaknesses, opportunities, and threats) analysis.

- **Relationship to past projects.** Have you ever done a similar project and, if so, was that effort supported by grant funding? This element of the project plan ensures that you review any past projects for mistakes that you can avoid or successes that you can capitalize on. It can also provide guidance for your funding research. DRI had previously gotten funding for training conducted through the community college, so the pursuit of funding through the college for its Lean Manufacturing and TS16949 training and implementation effort was documented on the project plan.
- **Budget summary.** You obviously have not identified the specific project budget, but you should be able to do a high-level budget. Support efforts such as tooling design or equipment specification do not need to be detailed in the project plan unless you have a good handle on those costs.

DRI developed the following budget summary as a result of the strategic planning meeting:

New grinding machine	$400,000
New mold for parts for the solar industry	$300,000
New packaging line for solar industry parts	$225,000
Total equipment investment	**$925,000**

Lean manufacturing training	$35,000
TS16949 quality system training and implementation	$40,000
Total training investment	**$75,000**
Total project investment	**$1,000,000**

- **Total project budget.** This is simply restating the total project investment. In DRI's case, the total project budget is one million dollars. Funders typically will ask for this number at the beginning of the grant application.
- **Specific line items.** Divide your project into major expense categories. This is helpful during the grant research process, as some funding programs will cover only training or only equipment. DRI chose to outline its specific line items in the following manner:

Equipment	$925,000
Training	$75,000

- **Research key terms.** Brainstorm with your team to come up with descriptive words for your project that can be used during your grant research efforts. The following are some prompts for the brainstorming process:
  - **Geographic focus.** Where will your project take place? You will want to identify the state, county, and city, as each of these geographic areas can be a source of funding.
  - **Area of interest.** What does your project address? Area of interest indicates what category of funding that a project may fall into, such as energy, or training.

These will be your keywords for the grant search, so, the more specific, the better. It is good to brainstorm potential areas of interest as a team. In the DRI case study example, some terms that the team developed were *renewable energy, continuous improvement, quality systems, job creation, job retention, equipment, employee training,* and *tooling.*

- **Types of support needed for project.** What type of support you would like to see from a funding organization. This, again, helps you narrow your search. Some examples from the DRI project are training, capital, and equipment. Other potential support areas for for-profit projects are technical assistance (if you want to use expertise from a company to accomplish the project goals) and in-kind support (if you are searching for a partner organization, such as a local university or vendor, to donate services or products to support the project).

Project definition is most definitely the most important, and most overlooked, part of the funding equation. Without a good project definition, you will spend a lot of time searching for grants that may not be a good fit, and you will struggle to complete a successful grant application.

Use the blank page at the end of this chapter to document some project ideas and some thoughts based on the content above.

Finding the Perfect Grant for Your Next Project

To understand the importance of the grant research process, consider the effects of an ineffective search for funding:

- wasted time
- funding not aligned with the project goals
- money "left on the table" because you didn't find the best funding source

Grant research is as important, if not more so, than the actual writing process. If you don't find the perfect grant for your project, you may waste time, money, and effort completing a grant application that gets denied.

———

How do you know if you have found the perfect fit? This is where your strategic plan comes in! If you have done your due diligence during a strategic planning process, you have identified your strengths, weaknesses, opportunities and threats. You have also identified your mission and your core values. If your strengths, mission, values and the project for which you are seeking funding align with the mission of the funding organization and the goals of their program, you likely have found a good fit. If any part of the program focus is at odds with your mission, values and strengths, you will waste your time putting together an application that will likely not be funded.

I would like to make two key points here:

- When I say that your project aligns with the funder's focus, I don't mean that it will align if you change a part of your program or if you stretch your core values or mission. I talk about this more in the Tips and Tricks section, but it bears repeating here. This is a trap that MANY companies fall into. Don't pursue funding that is at odds with what you company stands for. Don't change a project to get funding. Don't try to fit a square peg into a round hole!

- Just because you find a good fit from one funder, don't assume that a similar organization or program from the same funder will also be a perfect grant fit. Funding priorities and goals differ from one funding organization to another, even if their mission seems similar. Priorities and goals can also vary within a funding organization. Make sure you know what your project is trying to accomplish and what your strengths are. Check the guidelines and eligible activities on the grant announcement or funder's page and find the best fit.

———

Where do you find grant funding? In the age of instant information via the Internet, it is easier than ever to find sources of grant funding. The problem now is *too much* information. If you search for "grant funding" on Google, you get 266 million results! If you narrow your results by searching "grant funding, equipment," you are down to only 40,400,000 possible sources! Imagine how long it would take for you to click 40 million links!

Fortunately, there are many free or inexpensive ways to narrow the search and more quickly find the perfect grant:

- **Local economic development and city management departments.** In many cases, counties and cities may receive grant funding to help fund infrastructure and business development projects. I recommend that you get to know your alderman, your city and county economic development contacts, and the mayor of your city very well. Take them on a tour of your business, and contact them when you are planning any new project. If your voice isn't heard, the funding that they receive can and will be allocated to other city or county projects or to other companies for their improvement efforts.

- **E-mail.** This may seem way too simple, but I am all for simplicity! The reality is, sometimes you can find grant funding opportunities by e-mailing contacts in your network or equipment vendors. Maybe someone you know has gotten funding for a similar project, or your vendor has installed equipment for a grant-funded project.

- **Competitor sites.** Look at the "what's new" or news sections on websites of other companies in your industry or service sector. Many times, companies will advertise the receipt of grant funding, particularly if the award is for a large amount of money.

- **State economic development websites.** This is a particularly good idea if you are a for-profit company looking for grant funding. To find the economic development website, go to your state's website (www.illinois.gov for Illinois, similar format for other states) and do a search for "economic development." You can also do a search for "grants" on those websites, and you will likely find for-profit grant opportunities.

- **Google.** Speaking of Internet searches, you can also do a Google search for "grant for (your project name)." You must be willing to wade through pages of results, but if you are so inclined, this is a viable option.

- **Blogs and newsletters.** Many grant writers post grant opportunities daily via blog posts or newsletters. DH Leonard Consulting's Daily Dose of Grants and JM Grants' Daily Grant Gear are great examples of blogs and newsletters that provide information on funding programs.

- **Twitter and other social media.** Many grant writers and associations will tweet grant opportunities. I commonly do so through my Twitter feed (@lakeviewgrants). Search for "grants" on Twitter, LinkedIn, or Facebook, and you will find lots of other great resources.

- **Associations.** Trade and industry associations will often post grant opportunities on their websites as a service to their members.
- **Fund-raising associations and grant writing associations.** Not only can you get connected to great grant opportunities through organizations like the Grant Professionals Association (GPA) and the Association of Fundraising Professionals (AFP), you can also learn from workshops, webinars, and meetings that they offer. GPA offers its webinars to nonmembers, some geared to the for-profit community, for a very nominal fee.
- **Grants.gov.** This remains the primary resource to find any type of grant funding offered through the federal government. Once you register, you can even get grant opportunities e-mailed to you based on your preferences. You can search by keywords or funding source on their website.
- **Online grant research databases.** The best and most efficient way to do a targeted search for funding, particularly for grants offered through foundations, is to search online databases. Foundation Center and Grant Station are the two databases that I primarily use. You can find funding specifically for for-profit companies on these websites. Many major libraries also have a free copy of the Foundation Center Professional Package, which is the highest level package. Library patrons at most public libraries can use this database for free. If you purchase a package, the subscription can be as much as $1,200 per year.

One note: If you do choose to conduct your own research using the Foundation Center database, I highly recommend watching the tutorial video. The database has a lot of capabilities, and you don't want to miss out on any of them due to lack of familiarity with the site.

—

To maximize the effectiveness and consistency of your grant research efforts, I recommend using the project description template that you developed earlier in this chapter. This document will provide invaluable information for your searches, particularly for search keywords.

Here are some other tips for conducting effective research:

- Do your searches on a regular basis. If you don't find funding the first time you look, keep looking! Political priorities or endowments to colleges can change the funding landscape, so it is important to repeat the research process.
- Keep a log of funding opportunities found, whether they were pursued, and the result of the effort. This can be additional information kept on the project description document, or you can easily create an Excel spreadsheet with the same information.
- Keep your team apprised of funding opportunities and deadlines.
- Employ someone with grant research expertise on a freelance basis to save you the time and effort of doing this work, particularly if you don't feel you can keep up with it or don't have the tools to effectively do the research.

—

DRI took the templates that they developed for all of their projects and handed them off to the grant writer whom Sue hired to do the research. While Sue considered saving the money that was being paid to the grant writer by doing the research herself, she realized that neither she nor her staff had the time, expertise, or tools to do the research effectively.

After taking the time to thoroughly research the funding sources and discuss the situation with local and state economic development professionals, the grant writer came back with good news: DRI was eligible to apply for funding from various sources for their projects! The potential sources of funding included:

- **The state recycling program.** Since the reground plastic will be reused for manufacturing a product, the state's recycling program may cover a portion of the costs.
- **The state economic development department.** Since DRI plans to hire twelve new employees, and the capital investment in the tooling for the new solar equipment is substantial, the state's economic development department is going to consider offering an incentive package to fund a portion of the purchase as well as some of the employee training.
- **The community college.** The local community college was awarded a training grant to provide training to increase employee skills at companies in the college district. Since DRI is training internal auditors through the community college, they may qualify to receive a 50 percent discount on these training services.
- **An industry trade association.** It appears that, by joining an industry trade association, DRI might have access to grant funding to offset the cost of the Lean Manufacturing training.

The grant writer reviewed the research results with the team, who then happily gave the grant writer the approval to move forward with funding applications.

NOTES

Chapter 3

ELEMENTS OF A TYPICAL

GRANT APPLICATION

While DRI chose to employ a grant writer to write and submit their application, and you may choose to do so as well, it is important to know the basic elements of every grant application. If you are going to attempt to write an application yourself, the need is exponentially greater.

Grant writing is a collaborative process, with the grant writer or project leader working alongside a cross-functional team (as outlined in chapter 2). Each section of the grant application contains required elements. It is up to the team members to research and obtain information to satisfy those requirements. Basic knowledge of the elements of a grant application and the purpose of each element will greatly improve the chances of an effective and efficient writing process and receipt of grant funding to reward your efforts.

———

Element 1: Basic Demographic and Company Information

All grant applications will start by asking some basic questions about the applicant organization. Depending on the funding source, these can include:

- legal company name;
- address;
- Dun and Bradstreet, or DUNS, number;
- federal employer identification number (FEIN);
- number of employees, both at your location and corporate-wide;
- annual sales;
- website; and
- project contact name, e-mail address, and phone number.

You *must* fill in any information requested. I have found that the human resources or finance departments can be very helpful when completing this section. If you can't find the information (such as your DUNS number of FEIN), contact the funder's program manager. He or she can help you or can direct you to the appropriate resource.

Element 2: Abstract or Project Summary

The abstract (otherwise known as the project summary) is a synopsis of the application. If you receive funding, the project summary may be used for press releases. Even though this is one of the first sections in an application, it is typically one of the last ones completed. This is because the information needed for this section is included in the narrative and the budget elements of your finished proposal.

The abstract typically has word count limits, so my recommendation is to copy succinct statements from your project's purpose, cost, project activities, and anticipated benefits from your completed application into a Microsoft Word document and add text to make it flow. Use the character/word count feature at the bottom of the Word screen to check the number of characters or words in your document. If you find yourself with too many words or characters, edit the document until you have the correct number or less. When you have the appropriate number, copy and paste the final abstract into the proposal document. Just make sure not to delete anything important!!

Element 3: Introduction of the Organization

In this section, you will describe the company's history and products or services. If you have a short, interesting story about your company, put it in this section. Stories can help capture the application reviewer's attention. You can also describe key management team or staff project members; your company's mission, goals, philosophy, and success stories; and other facts that can establish your credibility with the funder. Any expertise that would lead to successful project outcomes should be outlined in this section as well.

Element 4: Purpose Statement

The purpose statement contains specific information about the outcomes, goals, and objectives of your project. The goals and objectives can be gleaned from your strategic plan or your project plan. The outcomes are what will change for your company, your customers, and the economy as a result of your project.

Element 5: Statement of Need

What drove you to undertake this project? What need will be met once the project is complete? The content for this section can be gleaned from the strategic plan's SWOT (strengths, weaknesses, opportunities, and threats) analysis or from the project plan. Any funded project must address a need that is consistent with the funder's goals, so this is a particularly important section.

Element 6: Project Methods or Procedures

This section is where you will get into the nitty-gritty of your project. A well-documented and well-presented project plan is necessary for this element of the grant application. You will discuss the basic project steps, who will be responsible for overseeing the project or ensuring its success, and a timeline for project completion. Sometimes the funder will have a particular format that needs to be followed for this section.

Element 7: Sustainability

How will you ensure that the project continues to provide benefits after the funding is spent? Funders will not provide money to companies who cannot assure them that they will not only use the money for its intended purposes but will continue to support the project after funds are spent.

Element 8: Evaluation

In order to show funders that your program was successful and that you recognize your project's strengths and weaknesses, you must have an evaluation plan. This plan identifies how you will measure progress toward the project goals and objectives during the project and toward the outcomes at the end of the effort. You identified specific project goals and outcomes in element four. You will add x number of jobs, or you will eliminate y percent of greenhouse gas emissions. If you achieve those goals, your project is successful. In your evaluation plan, you will specify how you will come up with the data to measure your progress toward your goals and will usually state your intent to provide timely progress reports as required by the funder.

Element 9: Qualifications and Personnel

Funders don't give money to organizations that they don't trust to spend the money wisely. Grant applications typically request an organizational chart and a list of key personnel who will be involved with the project. You must also list each person's qualifications as they pertain to successful project execution or may be asked to include their resumes.

If you have a history of successful grant management and reporting, mention that in this section. You are trying to assure funders that you are worthy and capable of receiving and managing their money.

Element 10: Budget

How much money do you want? If it only were that simple.

Most grant applications will request a line-item budget and will specify the budget categories. Equipment and labor are the two primary categories for equipment funding. You don't need to list each specific piece of equipment in the budget, but you may be asked to provide an attachment with more detail for some grant applications. These amounts can be estimates, but they should be based on two to three quotes from your equipment providers and a sound analysis of the labor involved, which should be conducted by your maintenance or engineering department personnel or your contractor prior to finalizing the estimate. Don't forget the preparatory work if you are installing equipment, or the cost of renting a room if you need one for training. The project team members should review your budget prior to submitting the proposal. You will be surprised how many budgets get changed during this review process.

I suggest using the highest bid and labor estimate for the grant application. It is very hard to request additional funds once you have received a grant, so aim high.

For training grant applications, the budget includes training hours, trainer cost, number of associates trained, a short course description, and average wage per trainee.

For grants that require a cash match from an applicant (and most do), the budget will have three columns. The first will be the amount of grant funding requested for that line item. The second will be the company cost share, and the third will be the line item total cost (the two other columns added together). Some spreadsheets will even automatically calculate the total cost when you complete the other elements.

Element 11: Attachments

The number and type of attachments are very specific to the type of funding requested. For state and federal funding programs, there are usually standard assurances, such as a drug-free workplace certification.

It is important that you carefully read the Request for Proposal and include all attachments required. These must be completed per the instructions and signed by a management representative (who may or may not be the project contact).

Congratulations! You now know the elements of any grant application and are ready to tackle the next one you encounter, right? Well, maybe.

If it seems overwhelming, that's because many grant applications are. It is not uncommon for a grant application and terms to exceed fifty pages.

This is where a good grant writer comes in very handy. Sue at DRI employed a grant writer, who helped her in the following ways for each grant application:

- She acquired all needed information for element 1, including the organization's DUNS number (which no one in the company knew).
- She led the team during the application process. This included establishing a timeline to ensure that the elements needed for a successful application were completed on time, as well as holding regular team meetings to address issues affecting timely submission.
- She interviewed management and team members and reviewed the company website for the purpose of obtaining information to write the introduction to the organization (element 3).
- She helped the team outline a project plan, including the purpose statement (element 4), statement of need (element 5), project methods (element 6), and sustainability plan (element 7). The grant writer turned this information into an eloquently written project narrative that met each funder's guidelines.
- She developed an evaluation plan based on the anticipated project goals, objectives, and outcomes (element 8).
- She obtained the résumés of key project personnel for element 9, along with budget information (element 10), and transferred that data into the format required by the funding entity.

- She collected signatures and information for required attachments (element 11). This required explaining to company management the need for financial statements and assurances (as a private company owner, Sue was a little reluctant to provide financial data to the funders).
- She acted as the project contact. As such, the grant writer answered all funder questions in a timely manner and responded to all team members' and managers' questions with the same timeliness. This relieved Sue of the responsibility, which she greatly appreciated, given the demands on her schedule.

The fee that the grant writer charged paled in comparison to the benefits realized above. Her involvement saved the company time and preserved their resources so that they could continue to address their customers' needs.

NOTES

Chapter 4
GRANT WRITING TIPS AND TRICKS

Before we move on, let me refresh your memory on the funding equation:

P + R + A = $

P refers to a well-defined **project**.
R refers to grant **research**, and more specifically, *effective* grant research.
A refers to a well written grant **application**.
$ equals money for your **project**

You have learned how to define your project and assign a project contact.

You have learned how to conduct effective grant research.

And you have learned the elements of a grant application.

By using the information learned in this book (and getting help where you need it), you will be able to access funding for your next project. However, I wouldn't feel right if I didn't send you on your way with a few tips and tricks to make the process easier.

—

Tip 1: Keep a file (hard copy or electronic) or binder with all pertinent grant information.

The file or binder should include a copy of the completed application, correspondence to or from funders or project vendors any invoices or financial documentation for future audits, notes from project meetings, and any other documentation pertinent to the project. This will come in handy in the event of an audit or a future application for similar work.

—

Tip 2: Read through a request for proposal (RFP) carefully before you even consider applying.

A grant program may look like the perfect fit based on the snippet that you see online or in e-mail correspondence. Once you read through the full document, however, there may not be a good fit, or the reporting requirements may be more than you are willing to commit to. If necessary, have someone else review it as well to get another opinion before embarking on the application process.

—

Tip 3: If you are in doubt about whether you can commit to a statement in a grant application, take it out.

If I suspect that one of my clients is ambivalent about a statement in an application I write, I ask, "Is this realistic?" If the client still hesitates or says no, I take it out. Be aware of the fact that this one simple move may disqualify you from funding, but it is better to take this route than to commit to something that you can't live up to.

—

Tip 4: Don't try to fit a square peg in a round hole.

Make sure your project is a *great* fit for a funding program. For example, you are going to install equipment to serve the automotive market. A recycling program comes out and will help pay for the equipment. Unless you can prove that your machines can meet the requirements of the grant, don't try to stretch your project scope just to get the funding. It's tempting when money is involved, but don't do it. It leaves you open to the potential for falling short on the commitments in the agreement and subsequently having your funding revoked.

—

Tip 5: Have someone outside the project team read the completed application before submitting it.

An outsider's perspective is vital when completing a grant application. Someone who has not been involved with the process can look at the content critically and question statements that you or your team may have made but that weren't caught during your internal review of the application.

—

Tip 6: Give yourself enough time to complete the application process.

As you can see from the content in the previous chapters, there is a lot of effort and time involved in the application process. *I suggest allowing at least two months prior to the grant program deadline* to properly collect data, ask questions, assemble a team, get quotes for equipment or training, compile the application, and conduct a proper review before submission.

Tip 7: Use technology to facilitate the grant application process.

I use Nozbe as my task manager(www.nozbe.com). I can access it from anywhere or any of my devices. It has a beautiful feature (as do other programs, such as Basecamp or Google Drive) that allows easy collaboration with other associates on your team. This can avert the need for excessive meetings, long e-mails, or lengthy phone calls. Technology can be especially helpful when you have team members scattered throughout the country or the world.

Tip 8: Get help from experts.

You have business to attend to. While I have written this book to provide you with information about grant writing and research, my goal was not for you to go out and do it (although you are certainly welcome to try). Rather, my goal, as stated in the introduction, is to help you to understand the process and your role in it.

To properly find grant funding and complete a grant application, you need to work in concert with an expert. Properly qualified experts will work with you and your team to supplement your talents with theirs, with the goal of finding and accessing grant funds. Use your time to do what you do best by outsourcing this effort!

Tip 8a: Don't just get any help, either.

The Grant Professional Credentialed (GPC) designation behind a grant writer's name means that person has devoted years of work and study to the craft of grant writing and has shown competency in all areas of grant writing. You wouldn't trust just anyone off the street to heal you when you're sick, would you? You would want treatment from an MD or other certified medical professional. Why would you settle for less when thousands or millions of dollars, along with your company's reputation, growth, and transformation, are on the line?

NOTES

CONCLUSION

I hope you have found the information contained in this book to be beneficial. Most of all, I truly hope that, as a result of reading it, you are not intimidated by the grant research and writing process and consider pursuing grant funding to help fund your next significant training or equipment investment.

—

So, what ever happened to Sue and her company, DRI? Well, their investment in the grant writer paid off in spades! Here is a list of the funding they received for each of their projects:

Equipment/ Training Item	Equipment/ Training Cost before Funding	% Funding Received *	Cost after Funding
New grinding machine	$400,000	90%	$40,000
New tooling for solar industry parts	$300,000	50%	$150,000

New packaging line	$225,000	0%	$225,000
Employee training	$75,000	50%	$37,500
Total	$1,000,000		$452,500

* These percentages, though hypothetical, are based on my actual experience with these types of projects. The project that was not funded could not be shown to solely benefit the solar industry, which is a common reason for denial of targeted industry funding requests.

The grant writer (who, by the way, was a GPC) charged DRI twenty-five thousand dollars to research and apply for this funding. After accounting for the cost of the grant writer, Sue's investment was reduced by $427,500, or nearly 43 percent. This almost doubled Sue's ROI and allowed for purchase of all this equipment.

As a result of the equipment purchase, Sue and her company had a 40 percent increase in sales the year after the investment and hired fifteen new employees (three more than anticipated). Not only did DRI benefit through increased revenue and profits and a greater reputation for social responsibility, but the local economy also benefitted from an increased tax base lower unemployment rates, and increases in employee investment and spending.

Truly a happy ending, and one that you and your company can experience as well.

———

Contact me, and we'll explore the possibilities together!

Micki Vandeloo, GPC
Lakeview Consulting
www.lakeviewconsulting.net
618-977-8570
Micki@lakeviewconsulting.net

www.ingramcontent.com/pod-product-compliance
Lightning Source LLC
Chambersburg PA
CBHW051224170526
45166CB00005B/2031